B♭ TRUMPET **Book 3**

D1398411

ACCENT ON ACHIEVEMENT

Mark
Williams

The "Keys" to Success: Progressive Technical & Rhythmic Studies in all 12 Major and 12 Minor Keys

Dear Band Student:

Congratulations on completing the first two books of
ACCENT ON ACHIEVEMENT. Book 3 will help you to develop the
musical and technical skills necessary for a lifetime of great music-
making. Your "Keys" to success include scales, exercises and
fun tunes in all 12 major and 12 minor keys. You'll learn new
rhythms and meters, and also improve your tone and intonation
while playing a rich variety of chorales. With diligent practice,
there's no end to what you can accomplish! We wish you the
best in your quest for musical excellence.

John O'Reilly   *Mark Williams*

John O'Reilly   Mark Williams

Instrument photos (cover and page 1) are courtesy of Yamaha Corporation of America.

ACCENT ON CONCERT B♭ MAJOR

CHORALE: CHILDREN'S PRAYER from "HANSEL AND GRETEL"

Engelbert Humperdinck
(1854–1921)

C MAJOR SCALE (CONCERT B♭)

INTERVAL WORKOUT

SCALE STUDY

CHROMATIC SCALE

ACCENT ON RHYTHM: 9/8 Time

6 Count: 1 2 3 4 5 6 7 8 9

MORNING HAS BROKEN

Irish Folk Song

Moderato

7 *mp* < *mf* > < *mf*

mf > *mp* <

ACCENT ON RHYTHM: 12/8 Time

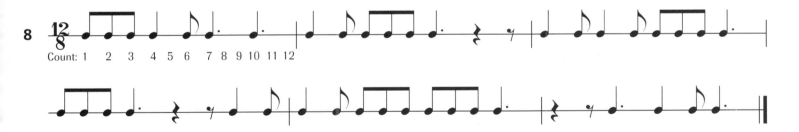

8 Count: 1 2 3 4 5 6 7 8 9 10 11 12

ANDANTE CANTABILE from "SYMPHONY NO. 5"

Peter I. Tchaikovsky
(1840–1893)

9 *mp*

ACCENT ON CONCERT G MINOR

CHORALE: BASED ON A THEME BY NEUMARK

Johann Sebastian Bach
(1685–1750)

Andante

10

mf *mp*

mf

rit.

A MELODIC MINOR SCALE (CONCERT G)

11

INTERVAL WORKOUT

12

*See Fingering Chart on page 38.

SCALE STUDY

13

A HARMONIC MINOR SCALE (CONCERT G)

14

ACCENT ON RHYTHM: $\frac{3}{2}$ Time

15

Count: 1 & 2 & 3 (e) & a

RONDO

Henry Purcell
(1659–1695)

Maestoso

16

THE WILD HORSEMAN

Robert Schumann
(1810–1856)

Allegro

17

ACCENT ON CONCERT E♭ MAJOR

CHORALE: BE THOU MY VISION

Traditional Irish Melody

Moderato

F MAJOR SCALE (CONCERT E♭)

INTERVAL WORKOUT

SCALE STUDY

CHROMATIC SCALE

ACCENT ON RHYTHM: ♪♩.

THE KEEL ROW

English/Scottish Folk Song

Allegretto

ACCENT ON RHYTHM: ♪♪♩♩ and ♪♪♪♩♪♪

PETITE OISEAU

Traditional

Moderato

ACCENT ON CONCERT C MINOR

CHORALE: PRELUDE IN C MINOR

Frèdèric Chopin
(1810–1849)

D MELODIC MINOR SCALE (CONCERT C)

INTERVAL WORKOUT

SCALE STUDY

D HARMONIC MINOR SCALE (CONCERT C)

ACCENT ON RHYTHM:

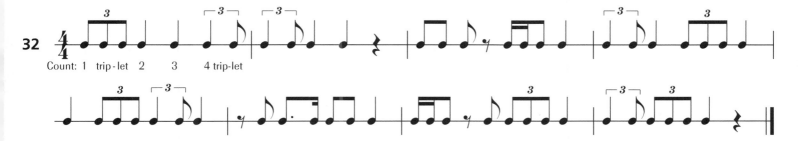

Count: 1 trip-let 2 3 4 trip-let

THREE WAYS TO SWING IT

Allegro

Swing feel

ACCENT ON RHYTHM: *Swing Eighth Notes*

Swing feel

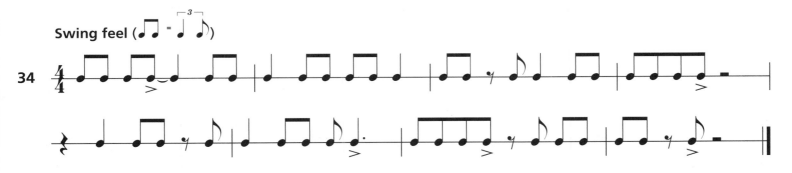

THE BATTLE OF JERICHO

Allegro - Swing feel

American Spiritual

Fine

D. C. al Fine

ACCENT ON CONCERT F MAJOR

CHORALE: SINE NOMINE

Ralph Vaughan Williams
(1872–1958)

G MAJOR SCALE (CONCERT F)

*See Fingering Chart on page 38.

INTERVAL WORKOUT

*See Fingering Chart on page 38.

SCALE STUDY

CHROMATIC SCALE

ACCENT ON RHYTHM: ♪♪ in 6/8 Time

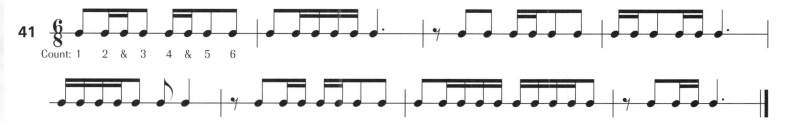

41 Count: 1 2 & 3 4 & 5 6

THE IRISH WASHERWOMAN

Traditional

42 Allegro
mf

LIP SLUR/FLEXIBILITY STUDY

43 *mp*

ACCENT ON CONCERT D MINOR

CHORALE: PICARDY

17th Century French Melody

ACCENT ON RHYTHM: ♩. ♫♩ in 6/8 Time

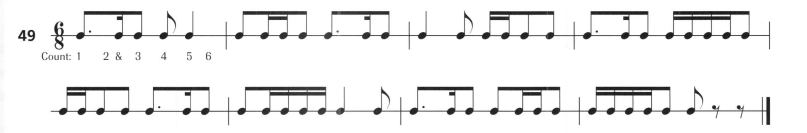

49

Count: 1   2 &   3   4   5   6

GREENSLEEVES

English Folk Song

Andante

50

mp   *mf*   *mp*   *mf*   *mp*

ACCENT ON RHYTHM: ♪ (Sixteenth Rest)

51

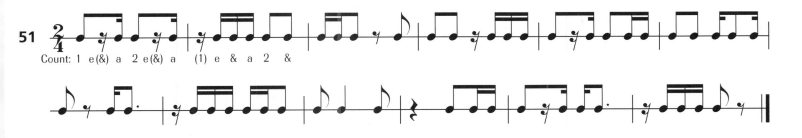

Count: 1 e (&) a   2 e (&) a   (1) e & a   2 &

LA CUMPARSITA

G. Matos Rodriguez
(1897–1948)

Moderato

52

mf   *f*

ACCENT ON CONCERT A♭ MAJOR

CHORALE: HOW FIRM A FOUNDATION

Early American Melody

*See Fingering Chart on page 38.

INTERVAL WORKOUT

SCALE STUDY

CHROMATIC SCALE

*See Fingering Chart on page 38.

ACCENT ON RHYTHM: 5/4 and 6/4 Time

58

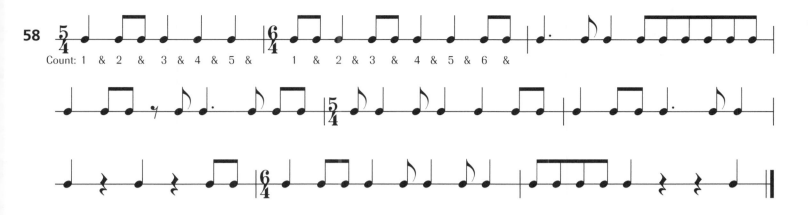

Count: 1 & 2 & 3 & 4 & 5 & 1 & 2 & 3 & 4 & 5 & 6 &

PROMENADE from "PICTURES AT AN EXHIBITION"

Modest Mussorgsky
(1839–1881)

Moderato

59

WALTZ from "SYMPHONY NO. 6"

Peter I. Tchaikovsky
(1840–1893)

Allegretto

60

ACCENT ON CONCERT F MINOR

CHORALE: THE GOD OF ABRAHAM PRAISE

Hebrew Folk Song

Moderato

61

G MELODIC MINOR SCALE (CONCERT F)

62

INTERVAL WORKOUT

63

*See Fingering Chart on page 38.

SCALE STUDY

64

G HARMONIC MINOR SCALE (CONCERT F)

65

ACCENT ON RHYTHM:

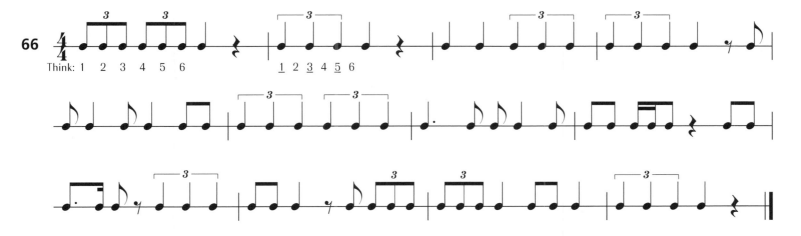

66

Think: 1 2 3 4 5 6   1 2 3 4 5 6

SOMETIMES I FEEL LIKE A MOTHERLESS CHILD

American Spiritual

67 Largo

TRIPLET TUNE

Maestoso

68

ACCENT ON CONCERT C MAJOR

CHORALE: IT IS WELL

Phillip Bliss
(1838–1876)

D MAJOR SCALE (CONCERT C)

INTERVAL WORKOUT

SCALE STUDY

CHROMATIC SCALE

ACCENT ON RHYTHM: *Changing Meters — $\frac{2}{4}$ through $\frac{6}{4}$*

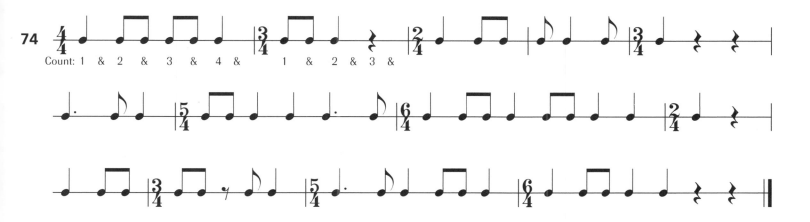

74

Count: 1 & 2 & 3 & 4 & 1 & 2 & 3 &

SOLILOQUY

75 Andante

mp

mf *mp*

mf

LIP SLUR/FLEXIBILITY STUDY

76 *mf* 1 3

2 3

1 2

1

2

0

1 2

ACCENT ON CONCERT A MINOR

CHORALE: BASED ON A THEME BY HASSLER

Johann Sebastian Bach
(1685–1750)

B Melodic Minor Scale (Concert A)

INTERVAL WORKOUT

SCALE STUDY

B Harmonic Minor Scale (Concert A)

ACCENT ON RHYTHM:

82

Count: 1 & 2 (e&) a 3 & 4 &

PRELUDE from "L'ARLESIENNE"

Georges Bizet
(1838–1875)

Allegro

83

CAPRICE No. 24

Nicolo Paganini
(1782–1840)

Allegretto

84

ACCENT ON CONCERT D♭ MAJOR

CHORALE: LONDONDERRY AIR

Irish Folk Song

E♭ MAJOR SCALE (CONCERT D♭)

INTERVAL WORKOUT

SCALE STUDY

CHROMATIC SCALE

ACCENT ON RHYTHM: Changing Meters — 6/8 and 2/4

90

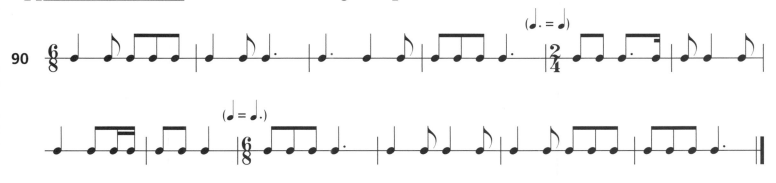

WASSAIL SONG

Traditional Carol

Allegretto

91

ACCENT ON RHYTHM: Changing Meters — 6/8 and 3/4

92

FIESTA MARIACHI

Allegro

93

ACCENT ON CONCERT Bb MINOR

CHORALE: KOMM, SÜSSER TOD

Johann Sebastian Bach
(1685–1750)

C MELODIC MINOR SCALE (CONCERT Bb)

INTERVAL WORKOUT

SCALE STUDY

C HARMONIC MINOR SCALE (CONCERT Bb)

ACCENT ON RHYTHM: $\frac{5}{8}$ Time

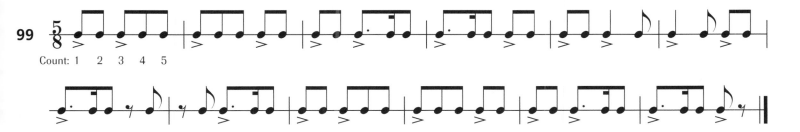

99

Count: 1 2 3 4 5

FUN WITH FIVE

Moderato

100

ACCENT ON RHYTHM: Changing Meters with $\frac{3}{8}$, $\frac{5}{8}$

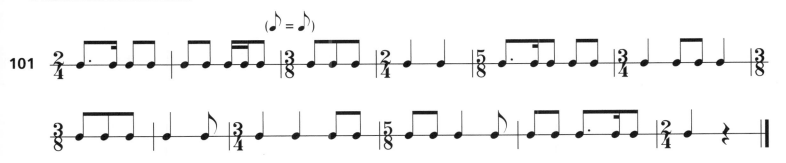

101

VARIATIONS ON A STAR SONG

Moderato

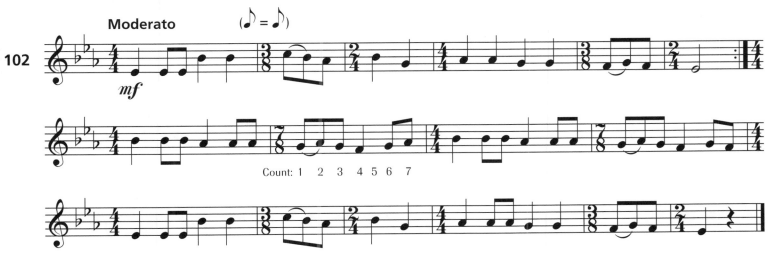

102

Count: 1 2 3 4 5 6 7

ACCENT ON CONCERT G MAJOR

A MAJOR SCALE (CONCERT G)

INTERVAL WORKOUT

CHROMATIC SCALE

LA CUCARACHA

Mexican Folk Song

Allegretto

AULD LANG SYNE

Scottish Folk Song

Andante

Fine

D.S. al Fine

ACCENT ON CONCERT E MINOR

F# MELODIC MINOR SCALE (CONCERT E)

108

INTERVAL WORKOUT

109

F# HARMONIC MINOR SCALE (CONCERT E)

110

LA CINQUANTAINE

J. Gabriel-Marie
(1852–1928)

111

Allegretto

ACCENT ON CONCERT G♭ MAJOR

A♭ MAJOR SCALE (CONCERT G♭)

112

INTERVAL WORKOUT

113

CHROMATIC SCALE

114

MICHAEL, ROW THE BOAT ASHORE

American Spiritual

Andante

115

mp

MARCH OF THE MEN OF HARLECH

Welsh Folk Song

Moderato

116

f

ACCENT ON CONCERT E♭ MINOR

F MELODIC MINOR SCALE (CONCERT E♭)

117

INTERVAL WORKOUT

118

F HARMONIC MINOR SCALE (CONCERT E♭)

119

THEME from "SWAN LAKE"

Peter I. Tchaikovsky
(1840–1893)

120

ACCENT ON CONCERT D MAJOR

E MAJOR SCALE (CONCERT D)

121

INTERVAL WORKOUT

122

CHROMATIC SCALE

123

ALLELUIA

Moderato   17th Century Melody

124

SHENANDOAH

Adagio   American Folk Song

125

ACCENT ON CONCERT B MINOR

C♯ MELODIC MINOR SCALE (CONCERT B)

126

INTERVAL WORKOUT

127

C♯ HARMONIC MINOR SCALE (CONCERT B)

128

HATIKVAH

Israeli National Anthem

Maestoso

129

p

mp

f

rit.

ACCENT ON CONCERT A MAJOR

B MAJOR SCALE (CONCERT A)

130

INTERVAL WORKOUT

131

CHROMATIC SCALE

132

BINGO

American Folk Song

Allegro

133

MY BONNIE LIES OVER THE OCEAN

Traditional

Moderato

134

ACCENT ON CONCERT F♯/G♭ MINOR

G♯ MELODIC MINOR SCALE (CONCERT F♯)

135

*Double-sharp: Raises the pitch of a note two half steps. (F double-sharp = G natural)

INTERVAL WORKOUT

136

G♯ HARMONIC MINOR SCALE (CONCERT F♯)

137

THEME from "SCHEHERAZADE"

Nicolai Rimsky-Korsakov
(1844–1908)

138 Moderato

ACCENT ON CONCERT C♭ MAJOR

D♭ MAJOR SCALE (CONCERT C♭)

INTERVAL WORKOUT

CHROMATIC SCALE

THE BLUEBELLS OF SCOTLAND

Scottish Folk Song

Moderato

BEAUTIFUL DREAMER

Stephen Foster
(1826–1864)

Andantino

ACCENT ON CONCERT A♭ MINOR

B♭ MELODIC MINOR SCALE (CONCERT A♭)

144

INTERVAL WORKOUT

145

B♭ HARMONIC MINOR SCALE (CONCERT A♭)

146

HAVA NAGILA

Hebrew Folk Song

147 Allegro

ACCENT ON CONCERT E MAJOR

F♯ MAJOR SCALE (CONCERT E)

INTERVAL WORKOUT

CHROMATIC SCALE

HOME ON THE RANGE

American Folk Song

ACCENT ON CONCERT C#/Db MINOR

Eb MELODIC MINOR SCALE (CONCERT Db)

152

INTERVAL WORKOUT

153

Eb HARMONIC MINOR SCALE (CONCERT Db)

154

WE THREE KINGS

Traditional Carol

Moderato

155

TRUMPET FINGERING CHART

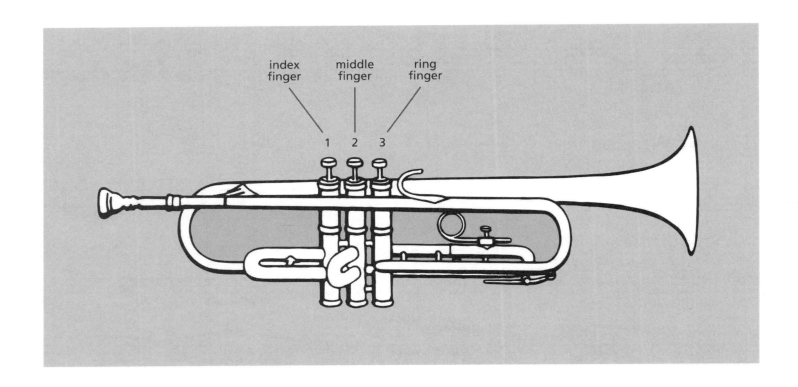

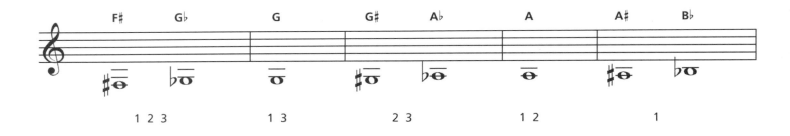

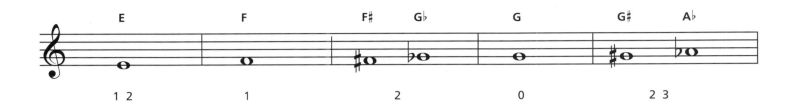

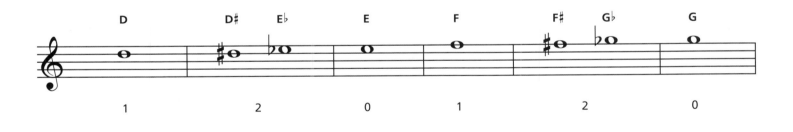

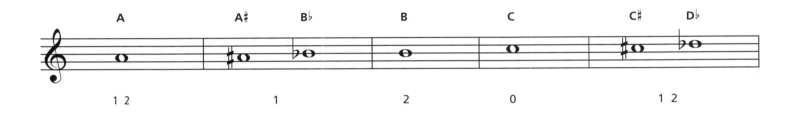

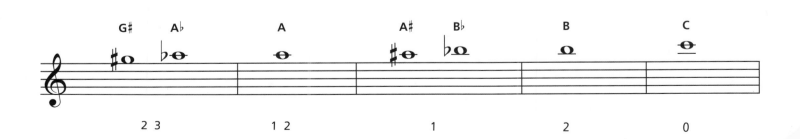

HOME PRACTICE RECORD

Week	Date	ASSIGNMENT	Mon	Tue	Wed	Thur	Fri	Sat	Sun	Total	Parent Signature
1											
2											
3											
4											
5											
6											
7											
8											
9											
10											
11											
12											
13											
14											
15											
16											
17											
18											
19											
20											
21											
22											
23											
24											
25											
26											
27											
28											
29											
30											
31											